An Epistle
on the Tripartite Nature of Man

Titles in the Series
Letters to the Devoted Follower of Christ

(in the order in which they were written)

AN EPISTLE TO THE MISERABLE
AN EPISTLE TO THE MODERATELY MISERABLE
AN EPISTLE ON JUDGMENT
ON THE TRIPARTITE NATURE OF MAN

An Epistle
on the
Tripartite Nature
of Man

By

A Little Anchor of the Church

Scriptures quoted from the King James Version (KJV) of the Bible. Please note that pronouns referring to God have been capitalized, though they are not in the KJV Bible.

The Little Anchor logo is derived from an image in the public domain and it and the name Little Anchor Books have no association with any other publishing company, nor was it intended they do so. By request, this volume was self-published.

ISBN-13: 979-8-3304-9115-5

An Epistle
on the
Tripartite Nature
of Man

To my much appreciated friend in Christ, who encourages me to continue on this high Path as much as I endeavor to encourage my friend —

Grace and peace to you with my prayers for your health, healing, and happiness.

You have expressed your wish to understand better what it means to be a living soul, or what it means to be of a tripartite nature — that is, of body, soul, and spirit. So I have written to the best of my ability some explanation of the matter insofar as I came to understand it. Please do not consider my words as the final word on any matter. If I write to you anything useful or edifying, may it be ascribed to God and His power to reveal. But if there are any inaccuracies or errors, let them be solely ascribed to me. I never intended to lead you or any other soul astray, only to help as I could. It is God's Truth that is important, not mine, if mine turns out not to be His.

Remember that as we speak of the life of the soul, anything we say is as a snapshot of it or of its relations with God. That is, our descriptions are but one frozen glimpse of life, and life itself is not in the picture but in the living, moving forms whose likeness the picture captured.

Regarding my continual use of the term *soul* when speaking of our fellow human beings, this letter will help explain why I refer to persons as such. It is not to avoid using gender terms in these days of unprecedented confusion.

For the most part it is a reference to the totality of person that God formed us to be, inclusive of all three parts, whether that be the soul growing in Christ or the one sunk low in its vices. Read what I have written, and I hope some of your questions will be answered. It is far too complex a subject for one letter, but I pray this will help lay a good foundation for later building from wherever God may bring you further illumination.

When I use the term *Man*, I do so as generally referring to a sentient, freewill species God created to interact with, and which encompasses the sexes. It is the person that comprehends incompletely who interprets this term to exclude women. It is we who misinterpret words and their meanings, not God, who always chooses His words with per-fection. I assure you, the species of Man includes both the masculine and the feminine. I capitalize it because it is the name of our species — a creation of God which He looked upon as having special purpose in the expression of His nature.

That historically Man has largely failed to express this divine nature well should not detract us from reminding ourselves of this purpose. I write this name as I do to remind myself to raise my gaze higher, to lift it from the bestial nature so often given free rein and to see in Man's beginning the pristine essence of a kind God made to have loving dominion over other life forms, to care for kindly and to respect what He chose of *His* own free will to create.

Man was created to be a counterpart to God — also why I capitalize the term, because it reminds me of the high God-and-Man relationship. He was created as an instrument of bringing God's good will into this earth, which had been affected so grievously by Lucifer's rebellion. And to Man was entrusted the well-being of this massive terrarium we call earth. Can his purposes be any higher? It is not intended to be an insensitive term, or to be anything less than inclusive of every human soul. God requires accountability and decency of behavior in all souls (or they may be

4

held accountable for the harm they have done to His creation), and He looks beyond sex and gender when dealing with spiritual matters (unless, of course, the point on which He is trying to instruct one is related to these some- how). Do not let the world's deliberately stirred-up confusion rob you of the degree of understanding you hope to obtain. Ignore those superfluous voices and set yourself to hear God.

We are of a kind, and the simplest and most-inclusive way to express this oneness of kind is to me to refer to our species as *Man*, the name of Adam in Scripture. The name *Adam* was given to the man as a personal name because it was also the name of his species. *Adam* means *mankind*. I hope this makes sense to you and is something you can accept for the sake of clarity.

I refer to the soul as *it* because the Word instructs us that in Christ there is neither male nor female.* No, I do not

---

* Galatians 3:28—"There is neither Jew nor Greek, there is neither bond nor free, there is

believe we become sexless in Heaven. But sex and gender are matters of flesh, whether fallen or unfallen. They often do not belong to issues of spirit, particularly as we are first developing in the Christ-life; and the use of *it* removes them from being issues on soulical or spiritual principles which apply to all souls. It pleased God to create the sexes,* so He is not just going to ignore what one is in the flesh. But His spiritual *principles* apply to all souls, and this is what I mean when I say certain issues do not apply—not because they do not matter, but because all are *encompassed* by these principles within God's standard for the species of Man.

These issues can seep into matters of soul but in themselves are of the flesh, as I think this letter will help explain why. To counter the confusion most seem to walk around with regarding spiritual things, it was simpler to remove gender from being an issue. You

---

neither male nor female: for ye are all one in Christ Jesus."
* See Genesis 1:27, 31; 2:20-25.

can read in many older volumes how the soul was referred to as a she: it was the human feminine as the counterpart to God's divine masculine. But I will say no more about this except to say that when my meaning might be mistaken (as is so often the case because people want complex subjects weakly distilled into only a few words), I prefer to apply the pronoun *it,* though even this is not a safeguard against all criticism. (For some are purposely set on mistaking our meaning because a spirit of antagonism against God compels them to do so. It is odd that they seem to believe so strongly in their personal ability to choose and we, blinded by our devotion to Christ, as those who do not think independently, when it seems they live enslaved to those forces which compel them and the soul who has found freedom in Christ does not.)

As to why I capitalize so many nouns—simply put, I capitalize most terms that express God's Essence, which is divine; or I capitalize them for clarity's sake because they are things so closely associated with God or His ways that I do not wish to be misunderstood. After all, Babel was our fault, not God's. That human language is such an imprecise form of communication is not because God did not give Man upon his creation a language that worked perfectly for him. We compromised its integrity by our determination to do things our way; and the consequence of this was the fracturing of what was inclusive into the hundreds of languages and their accompanying dialects we have today—and the freer the spirit of sin, the greater the fracturing it seems.

Let us be gracious one to another as we endeavor to express the truths God has revealed to us. One may be highly educated and yet has little spiritual understanding compared with the uneducated-but-spiritual souls he is speaking to. Let us not humiliate him any more than he ought to humiliate the man who holds the office of prophet yet has no higher education and whose proper grammar is noticeably lacking.

So the manner of my style is meant to clarify my meaning and to better honor the One about whom I write. I will keep to my way, and you express yourself as you feel led. If someone who might see this decides, "Well, if this is capitalized, then that should be too," he is entitled to his opinion. This was simply how I was led to express myself when I wrote this. Let us not become legalistic for the sake of a few characters in an imperfect language. If I have overlooked something I typically capitalize, it is no matter, since I utilize this method for clarity, and not because I am trying to make some kind of statement. May God bless you for endeavoring to seek out His Truth in all Its varied representations, accepting It in Its diverse expressions. It pleases God to utilize many different styles, the better to reach many different kinds of persons. It is the voice of the Shepherd we must be diligent to hear through these differing expressions of Truth.

And now, here is my brief explanation of the concept of being a tripartite being—of body, soul, and spirit—which has come to my aid significantly over the years. I sincerely hope it aids your understanding too.

There are many who would say that what happens in the inner person cannot be known with any clarity or that few concepts regarding spiritual growth make sense. This is not true, however. For the patient and sincere soul who desires to know the mind of God on these kinds of matters, it will soon find that it is not nonsense at all and that a great many invisible matters can be known with much clarity. One of these is the topic of what it means to be of a tripartite nature—that is, of three distinct parts.

To begin, Genesis 2:7 says that God created Man to be "a living soul." This verse explains to us that Man had a body which was formed from the dust of the earth. Then God "breathed into his nostrils the breath of life; and man became a living soul." Any such study will very probably begin here, because it is one of the most useful scriptural explanations of Man's composition. It may not seem like much at first, as the Word often does not. Holy Scripture reveals Its secrets as we seek knowledge of God according to His ways and time.

God is Spirit,* even though a great part of what He created is matter. Being all powerful, He has the ability to accomplish the creating of something from nothing—in this case, the creation of matter where there had only been spirit—His Spirit. This He did when He formed Man's body and the rest of creation. But when He breathed into Man, He was giving to him of His own life force, which is Spirit. Since God is also Love,† we can say this is why we connect with His Love on a spiritual level rather than a physical one, because God's Essence is as much Spirit as It is Love. It would be accurate to term His Essence as the Spirit of Love. So we seek union with His Spirit through our spirit.

---

* John 4:24

† I John 4:8—"He that loveth not knoweth not God; for God is love."

Yet this union expresses itself through the earthen vessel, the flesh, which requires the mediation of the soul. God chose to fashion us with a three-fold nature, and it is through the proper working of this nature that we are able to give the greatest expression of His image without Him violating our liberty to choose.

God created matter to illustrate to us principles of the spirit, which by His wisdom He chose to make less visible to us, particularly when we are not living in union with Him (for He does not wish to reveal certain things to those who would use any knowledge they could against His children). It is this union that reveals the spiritual reality as He intended it to be by His good will toward us. It became all but invisible to Man after his fall except when inappropriately invoked through occult means and by the purposed invasion of those who rebelled against God. Much of Man's ancient idolatrous practices seemed to have been taught him by these fallen ones, wherein we see much inversion of the divine principles. To respect why such practices are wrong involves studying the principles of union God provided to us for our clarity. Those who write off God's restrictions for us demonstrate how little real understanding they have of Him and His ways.

The invisible union between God and Man—which is the whole point in seeking understanding regarding our soul, that we may better understand our relationship with God—is founded on the spiritual principle of like being joined to like, which we fail to appreciate unless we comprehend the disparity between flesh and spirit. One is not just the part we see in the natural and the other what belongs to the invisible. They are two distinct parts of our nature. One is but a shadow of the other.

Consider these two references, one from the old covenant and one from the new: "Ye shall keep My statutes. Thou shalt not let thy cattle gender with a diverse kind: thou shalt not sow thy field with mingled seed: neither shall a garment mingled of linen and woollen come upon thee."* "Now this I say, brethren, that flesh and blood cannot inherit the kingdom of God; neither doth corruption inherit incorruption."†

We can only connect with God in our spirit because He established His creation to work on the principle of like joining to like. I am not trying to be legalistic about specific examples, and I do not advocate going to outward extremes, such as wearing only cotton. We can easily become distracted by material matters when the whole point of the illustration was to instruct us on the spiritual. [Rolls eyes at self.] If adhering to a physical practice helps you remember the spiritual principle behind it, by all means follow this practice until you remember the principle so well you don't need to rely on the practice anymore. But such adherence is personal; we should not put expecta-

---

* Leviticus 19:19

† I Corinthians 15:50

tions on others to follow the practices we do for our individual growth. Jesus had almost nothing but harsh criticism for Pharisees.

It is a very basic spiritual principle that says the fleshly part of us is separate from the spiritual, particularly since the fall from grace; and until one respects the truth of the principles which apply to us in this fallen state, God very well may not speak on those that apply to the redeemed state. The foundation stones are laid before the upper stories of the spiritual structure. This is not because God would have us forever dwell on being fallen; it is because we pridefully want to be promoted to secondary school when we have not mastered the learning of the elementary grades. If we are promoted just to satisfy our desire to be so, we soon find that we are not equipped to face the learning challenges of the upper grades. Humbleness is a challenge for most of us until we are relieved of this self and promoted to Heaven. Don't be too hard on yourself if you feel the struggle; just keep journeying toward God. But forgive my digression. One thing always leads to another.

The point is that flesh and spirit never were of the same kind, whether fallen or unfallen. They are two parts that do not directly mix. In the second verse quoted above, Paul includes both the unfallen state of flesh and blood, and the fallen state of corruption (which enveloped flesh and blood; but God created flesh and blood to serve a divine purpose, so by themselves they are not fallen). Neither of these human states was designed to enable one to inherit the spiritual kingdom of God. Both states require the intermediary help of the soul, and that is why we say our soul communes with God in our spirit, because this expresses how in this fleshly frame we still have access to God, who is Spirit in His Essence. He *chose* to take on human flesh and to become Emmanuel[*]; but God Himself is not flesh in His Essence; His Essence,

---

[*] Matthew 1:23

His natural state, is Spirit. This principle
of the soul's role of mediation between
flesh and spirit points us to the spiritual
reality that the soul and God require the
mediatory help of Christ. In this God-
Man relationship, Jesus became the Soul
that stands between Man (the flesh) and
God (the Spirit).*

---

* This principle is absolutely true regarding the
sin state—we can only presently be unified
with God through the mediation of Jesus
Christ and the sealing pact of His shed Blood.
But this principle was also in place even before
Adam fell from the state of grace, God just
founded His Way of Salvation for us upon it: for
Adam still had to choose to be bound to Spirit-
God in his own spirit, which required the
mediation of his soul since God had created
him to live in the flesh and to have the freedom
to choose how he would express the divine
image in this earth. So Jesus did not come into
existence because Man fell, even though God
made Him to be our Way of Salvation. The
three parts of God already existed, and would
have whether or not Man fell (and arguably we
consist of three parts because God does, and
this is part of being made in His image; our
three parts is how God chose to express His
Triune Being). Jesus was the Word of God sent
out into creation whenever God made a decree,
and it was this part of God that took fleshly
form, that of His own free will, consented to
become the mediatory Vessel needed to set
things right. So God has remained consistent
in His principle—and His principles do not

17

So Man has a body, and he has a spirit. Because he has both, and especially because the body is not more important than the spirit,* it would not be accurate to say that Man is, in totality of his person, a being of bodily form. Neither, though, would it be accurate to say that Man is a being of spiritual form. Certainly he is both, but he is not so preponderantly physical or spiritual that he can be classified as simply one or the other. He is always both all the time. Consequently, a new term is needed, one that encompasses what it means to be both body and spirit. This new name that describes succinctly the totality of both the physical and spiritual natures

---

change—of laboring within the three-fold nature He created us to have.
* II Corinthians 3:17-18—"Now the Lord is that Spirit: and where the Spirit of the Lord is, there is liberty. But we all, with open face beholding as in a glass the glory of the Lord, are changed into the same image from glory to glory, even as by the Spirit of the Lord." Paul did not make statements such as this because flesh is more important than spirit. And spirit is more important simply because God is Spirit and we are being transformed into what He is.

of Man is *soul*. When a person is called a soul, it signifies that he or she is both material and spiritual. They are both understood to be present when the term *soul* is applied (or they used to be) — the visible and the invisible conjoined in a unique entity.*

This term, however, also signifies the third part of Man. It is not merely the overall term that explains a two-sided nature. Man is called a tripartite being for a reason. He is the composition of three parts: spirit, soul, and body. He has a body and a spirit, but the word tripartite is used because he also has a soul. Soul does not only imply the totality of body and spirit: it also implies the *meeting together* of body and spirit. It

------

* Many argue about whether animals possess a soul. Certainly they possess unique personalities, and this may qualify as a special, invisible substance God planted in them upon their creation. That the animal soul must be the same as the human soul does not necessarily follow, however. It does seem clear that the human soul was uniquely created for relationship with the divine, whereas an animal's comparable relationship is with their persons. I.e., we seem to be as God to them—all the more to do the best we can by them.

becomes a part of the whole in its own right. It does this by consequence of the disparity between the body and the spirit, those parts being so different they need common ground to come together. The soul is that common ground. It is just as much a living organism that has the ability to develop and mature, to change and learn as it experiences life, as the body and spirit do, according to their different natures; but the soul does this as the expressive unity of the other two natures, thus creating a third aspect to a person's being that is unique in its own right.

The two parts, spirit and body, must at some point in existence interact, for they belong to the same time and place during the duration of this mortal existence. When this happens, the reaction cannot be accurately categorized as physical or spiritual, as it is as much one as the other. Both natures have played a part in this interaction, so there exists a third part of Man that is the encountering of the two other parts, and this part is the soul.

But do not be misled by the term *categorized.* The lines between the three parts of Man are not always easily defined — and some never become even slightly adept at defining them, more's the pity for them, for they exist all life long with only a modicum of self-awareness. Sometimes these lines are heavy and stark like a 20-foot-thick wall of stone that encompassed some ancient cities; but at other times are as the shore of the ocean, which, though not obliterated by the ebb and flow of the tides, moves slightly with them. Hence the need of God's active word, "the dividing asunder of soul and spirit, and of the joints and marrow,"* in order to rightly understand and regulate the boundaries between the parts.

The meeting of these two is not a joining in the sense that the essence of the one totally infuses the other. They each remain distinct so that a person always has a body as well as a spirit. If they mixed in all the essence of what

---

* Hebrews 4:12

they are, these two natures would cease
to be distinct, and then one new nature
would form from their merging; and
Man would arguably be a being of only
one part instead of three. Scripture
teaches otherwise, as does experience:
there are always occurrences which
demonstrate that not all can be explained by the body, nor can everything
be explained in spiritual terms. There *is*
more to a person than his flesh, and it is
quite obvious that even during encom-
passing spiritual experiences, the reality
of the body can hardly be ignored.

The soul is the common ground the
other two residents of the neighborhood
need to meet, because neither can visit
the other in their homes. It is as though
one breathes Aether and the other one
rich oxygen. Or perhaps it would help to
think of the spirit as a fish and the body
as a rabbit. They need an intermediary
who can give expression to the voice of
each. The soul, then, is the inner
functionary and the outward expression
of these exchanges. Picture it, arms
crossed, with one hand laying hold of

the spirit and the other grasping the flesh. It binds the other two to it, and all together they express the whole person. It is the middleman.

The soul represents the whole person because it speaks for both other parts which are unequipped to speak for one another. The spirit cannot speak for the body, as it has no experience of physical affairs; neither is the body able to speak for the spirit, having no conception of what it means to be spiritual, apart from what it learns through the soul. However, the soul can speak for both, as it has access to both parts and is able to touch and experience each to some extent. It is a kind of vessel that receives what each other part wants to pour into it. This is why its expression tends to reveal whether a person lives mostly of the spirit or of the flesh, for if it lives more of the flesh, more of this part overflows into the soul. And if the spirit of that person is not resurrected, then it has nothing to add to the vessel. This is why some physical acts feel like they are of the spiritual: it is not, as some believe, because the body and spirit have temporarily become one. It is because the soul, which is able to connect with spirit, can also partake of bodily experiences.

This is also why what we do in the body is such a serious matter to God — because He ever appreciates that physical acts have access to the spirit through the soul. There are dividing lines, but no materials hard enough to prevent the physical from seeping into the spiritual exist between our three parts. Like the blood whose elements reach to all parts of our body, so do the essences of our physical acts reach all parts of our inner self. It is a pity most of us do not learn this sooner, as then much time occupied with repentance and reformation might have been used for higher things. But God will not violate our freedom to do as we most desire, which is why He is so pleased with us when we finally do declare our desire is for Him.

The proper order of Man's nature is spirit, soul, and body. It does not signify in what order we state these parts or whether we provide those we encounter with more explanation than they were looking for at that moment. What matters is that we labor to recall to our self that God intended this to be the order of our nature to ensure the proper balance in our life of these various parts. And it is important to live what this means according to the degree of understanding we possess. (God does not require we possess understanding to which we are not yet capable of attaining. We sometimes, however, get called to task because there is understanding we had much opportunity to obtain but we chose to be about profitless activities instead. I speak of this from personal experience.)

So the classification and order that many give expression to human nature—of body, mind, and spirit—is somewhat erroneous. It reflects a lack of understanding about the true natures of body and soul, which need to be dominated (taken under the loving dominion) of the spirit. It categorizes all that is not body or spirit as belonging to mind, which omits one's struggles with heart and self-will—or it is classifying all these as being matters *of* mind, or perhaps it includes things of heart as belonging to spirit. Essentially, they treat the three equally insofar as I can tell. I do not believe they are, however, nor does the mind envelop all the various in-between parts, or God's Word would not distinguish them from one another.*

---

* For example, Psalm 26:2 separates the heart and mind—"Examine me, O LORD, and prove me; try my reins [or mind] and my heart." First Samuel 20:7 and Luke 22:22 are examples of persons exercising their will alternately in evil and in good. Arguably the mind and the will are interchangeable because it is largely in the mind that we justify our choices, which are a matter of self-will. But one can also see in some of the very young whose minds are only beginning to develop, a strong sense of self-determination, thus suggesting they are separate faculties. The point to remember is that there is an inner person that must be made subject to God's rule, or it will never develop in this lifetime into what He designed Man to become. However we divide up the inner parts, Scripture teaches that we do

Looking forward, we take hope in the promise that God has a resurrected body in store for His redeemed* that will effectually reconcile the parts of Man so that we will then live from a unified, central being, no longer divided in heart, mind, or soul. Some all but achieve this divine balance here on earth, and we can pray that a state of single-mindedness is a gift soon bestowed by God's grace upon His Church. In truth it already has been. It is part of our inheritance in Christ. But not all have received this part of Him yet. We develop in the Christ-life in increments, and some of us require more time on the road than others, due to disability or infirmity of soul. So let us not judge our fellows, as we cannot be

---

possess faculties of heart and mind and will, and that these belong to the soul of Man. The spirit also has its organic functions, but I am not speaking of these here. Most of Man's concepts on the soul are erroneous, just as classifying human nature as entirely physical or spiritual is erroneous. Man is a complex entity, as befits one made in God's image, and we still have a lot to learn.
* Consider I Corinthians 15:35-50.

aware of everything that might be hindering them from making speedier progress.

The complexity of our being is likely why many stumble upon which term to use as the part of us that goes to Heaven when we die in the flesh. Do we call this part the soul or just the spirit? As far as I can tell, either is acceptable. Certainly the spirit goes to Heaven to dwell with God, but part of the soul is of the spirit. In this sense the soul is the portion that developed due to the place where spirit brushed up against flesh; and since they cannot mix, as oil and water cannot, they each in a sense contributed to a new substance, much in the way oil and water are both used to create bread. The flesh is as water, and the spirit is as oil. Or you can exchange these if you like; the point is that they are separate substances that do not mix together just by themselves. The soul is as the flour that binds them together. So when they are mixed together with the soul and a few other substances, another article, bread, is produced — and here these other substances are God and His work in Man that enable us to become more than just two disjointed parts of body and spirit. Is the finished product of bread more like oil or more like water? It is not any closer in likeness to one than to the other. It is its own substance in its molecular composition.

So spirit having contributed to the composition of the soul, how can we declare the soul does not go to Heaven? Did the oil go to Heaven but not the bread it was part of? That makes no sense, especially since once the bread has been made, there is no way to remove the oil. And if there were a way to return the bread to its constituent elements, the bread would no longer exist. Why would God damage the bread (the soul) for the sake of taking the oil (the spirit) to Heaven? And as far as the body is concerned—well, God decreed this must fall back into dust.* Yet

---

* Genesis 3:19—"In the sweat of thy face shalt thou eat bread, till thou return unto the ground; for out of it wast thou taken: for dust thou art, and unto dust shalt thou return." There is not time here to explain why, having

clearly He "remembered that they were but flesh; a wind that passeth away, and cometh not again."* That is, He has not forgotten that part of us falls away for a time, as unremembered by the earthly as dust that blows in the wind. He remembers what we still await according to His promises to us. We must trust that He has good reason for everything He does, and He never errs.

As I believe you know, many satisfy themselves with saying the soul is the mind, the will, and the emotions; and this is most certainly true. I have no quarrel with such a definition. It has

---

been freed from the curse through the redemptive act of Christ, the flesh is still to fall to the ground but to say that the sin-tainted flesh is supposed to go into the grave just as Jesus did, and be raised to resurrection Life as He was. That God chose to divide the resurrection times for the spirit and the body is not our issue as devoted followers of Christ. This is the Way God made for His Life to fill our soul, and we choose to respect His Way or not. And His Way has decreed that the last enemy to be defeated is death (I Cor. 15:26).
* Psalm 78:39

helped many people, I am sure. (And I wish I had heard it myself long ago when I was trying to suss out these matters — though if I had I might have been satisfied with it and not come to greater understanding.) But why they belong to the soul and how the soul differs from the spirit is not fully explained by this definition. It is a succinct explanation that will help many beginners, so remember it and pass it along whenever you think it might help. I offer this larger explanation because you seemed to want more understanding than such a concise definition can give. Most persons will be satisfied with the short definition, so let it go at that. But you are always free to seek further illumination. If God does not wish to reveal something to us, He doesn't. It is as simple as this — although arguably we do not receive illumination because our level of faith is too low to receive it; yet there are things God reveals only at certain times. But to ask anything re-spectfully because you wish for more understanding is never wrong.

That the mind, the will, and the emotions belong to the soul portion of our nature are because one, they are all influenced by things of the flesh and given visible expression through the intermediary vessel; and two, they are given to us for our use upon our creation. That is, we are not barred from their use until we are redeemed. Consequently, they are not things of the spirit, which is not born into life until God buys us back from the kingdom of darkness, or the kingdom of death.* The spirit is breathed into resurrection Life as we are redeemed, and then the soul can be touched by this Life of God and have It transform its mind, heart, and will. Without this spiritual resurrection, these soul-faculties can only rise as high as is possible for Man to develop them on his own—which can be very high.

---

* In truth He already bought us all back through Jesus' finished work on the cross. But we have to choose of our own free will to have this purchase price applied to our spiritual account. So practically, for those who do not choose this, it is as though redemption did not happen. But Christ died once for all (I Peter 3:18).

But with God, there is no cap on what we can become. Without God's Essence imbuing us, we cannot exceed the boundaries of the kingdom of darkness. We can do our utmost to illuminate the gloom, but regardless how large a soul might appear, in the cosmic picture it is really only as a tiny candle by which one cannot even read, compared with the Light that casts no shadows and never sets. Moreover, it is a soul fueled by the energy of self rather than of Spirit.

Our freedom to choose is a matter of soul. This freedom to choose the ways we will go and how we will respond to God is bound up in our mind, our self-will, and the state of our heart. God permits us to feed these soul-faculties to whatever excess our self-determination directs and in whatever ways we so desire, and these ways never have to be of Him. He does not force us to become self-disciplined in our inner person or transformed into His likeness. He created Man with the full capacity to think, feel, and will for himself before he fell from grace. So we also have this capacity, though stained by the sinful nature. God does not revoke the gifts He gives.* He permitted Adam to pass along everything he could within the sin-state. What Adam could not pass on was a living spirit, and what he could pass on was tainted by sin. But God never made Man less because of sin. He created him to be a three-fold being, and he is still a three-fold being. Even unredeemed, Man still possesses a spirit; it just lies there dead and non-functional until the will chooses to have God breathe upon it. But God did not kill it; sin did.

So despite that redemption is needed to restore us to a functional three-fold nature, God made a Way to accomplish it that is as simple as receiving Jesus His

---

* Romans 11:29—"For the gifts and calling of God are without repentance." And lest you be tempted to correct me regarding context—that Paul was speaking regarding ancient promises God made to Israel—I reply without apology that sometimes we must look beyond these things and perceive the principles God has placed within the living illustrations Scripture provides us. These principles are the foundation upon which creation was established. We comprehend them because God gave them illustration through Man's history.

Son as that mediatory Soul between God and Man. (I cannot discuss presently how much is Man's will and how much God's grace. It would lengthen this letter considerably, and I wished to get it to you as soon as possible.)

God made a way for that pristine nature of Man to be recovered, in part now and fully resurrected later. Why He separated this redemption is according to His wisdom, but I remind you of this: "But God hath chosen the foolish things of the world to confound the wise; and God hath chosen the weak things of the world to confound the things which are mighty."* At the end of time, God will be revealed as One who was unhin-dered in the fulfillment of His Plan for Man by any weakness or vice of human nature the enemy could exploit. He will demonstrate for all creation that the

---

* I Corinthians 1:27. Consider also Hebrews 11:39-40—God has separated our resurrection into two parts because as far as the physical is concerned, He wished us all to partake of it together, because we are a single Body of believers.

weakness of Man did not keep Him from performing what He set out to accomplish, even though it can hinder individual souls from receiving all the eternal reward they might have if they had aspired to grow in Christ.

Inappropriately obtained strength of soul is why persons who have not yet been reborn in Christ are so compelled by one of these three faculties: the mind, the will, or the emotions. In not possessing a living spirit (only an in-the-grave one), the strength of their person is in soul only. Every bit of inner strength nurtured has gone to feed the soul, there being no living spirit-receptacle to receive the spiritual food and drink many do make the effort to feed themselves even when they are not reborn in Christ. And sadly this is also true of many who are reborn but who take no care to feed their spirit.

The spirit has something of an organic nature of its own, which expands and bends and grows (and contracts in seasons of famine so that we are not overcome by a giant maw seeking to devour whatever it can, such as during seasons when earthly tasks are so pressing we cannot draw away with God to a remote place to feed on the Bread of Life as much as we would like)—in short, it has the capacity to adapt to what it is fed and how much. If you feast your spirit on Christ, your spirit will develop into a vessel adequate to receive Him, and likewise your soul.

Trying to get your soul to process spirit-food is like expecting your intestinal tract to make use of undigested food without the aid of your stomach. The food is supposed to be largely broken down by the time it reaches the digestive tract. The soul cannot take in spirit-food until the spirit has first digested it into smaller pieces and made it ready to be absorbed by the soul. And then the earthen vessel takes this food to fuel the expression of its beliefs, through hands and feet and so forth. We largely see through a person's actions what is the state of his soul: "Ye shall know them by their fruits."*

Or, if you like, the unresurrected spirit starving for food inside these persons is like a little country store closed for business with a sign in the window that says, "Gone fishing." The store serves no one any practical purpose or profit. It stands ready to, though, and only needs opened for business. (But I am not saying God has anything against going fishing once the spirit has been fed.) Remember, these are just snapshots of the life of the soul. No statement can fully encompass the living forms of Christ and His relations with the soul. It must experience Him for itself.

Some souls become very well-developed, fit, and muscular inner persons who are on the spiritual battlefield as David's mighty men were on the physical one.† Their spirit has grown big and strong, and so then by

---

* Matthew 7:16
† II Samuel 23:8-39

extension does their overall soul. The outer person's appearance is insignificant. It can be a small frame, but when the spirit is mighty, it can help carry the physical frame. Though God would have us all be healthy and fit (I believe), He has also made a way for the body to receive strength through the spirit and soul when it needs to continue here to complete what He sent it to do but for whatever reason is oppressed by illness or injury.*

And some souls are weak, sickly entities with little spiritual drive. This is why some comment, "He's not very spiritual" (or people make such com-

---

* Great manifestations of healing have been prophesied to occur in the near future. That this healing was always available to us through Christ but countless persons were not able to partake of it, may be difficult for some to reconcile. But it may be one of those doctrinal errors God chose not to address in a corporate way before this time. Our trust in God these days has to be implicit. He is still the God of Romans 8:28—His will for us was never sickness and suffering, but they have occurred profusely in this earth; however, He is still able to bring good from all of it for those who love Him. Let us trust Him to follow through on His promise.

ments about themselves). But this is a misconception. We are all spiritual, the weak one as well as the strong. So we can declare, as Scripture teaches, "Let the weak say, I am strong."* This is because we are all rightly spiritual beings, and because in Christ we all have the potential of attaining to Christ's perfect inner nature — in increments so that God can never be accused of violating our self-will at any point along the way. It is only that some make no real effort to tone the inner man. But in Christ it is done, it is finished, as Jesus said on the cross.† By declaring it we declare according to the principle of Romans 4:17 — we declare what is not as though it already were.‡ The inner man has been birthed in Christ,§ and by

---

* Joel 3:10

† John 19:30

‡ Romans 4:17—"…even God, who quickeneth the dead, and calleth those things which be not as though they were." Consider all of chapter four of Romans, because this principle is illustrated through the faith of Abraham.

§ Here in the second birth we find both the masculine and the feminine—the Fatherhood and the Motherhood of God. For it is through

exercising its freedom to choose His
Spirit-food, it begins to grow, develop,
and finally mature. The one who
manifestly becomes more spiritual was
the one who declared his soul does
indeed have union with God through
Christ, is growing up to full maturity,
and will someday have its full redemption. We do not need to express it this
precisely, for God can discern the
deeper meanings within us. It is enough
to choose this growth experimentally
and trust Him to care for the soul as the
Loving Parent He is.

When we feed the spirit with the good
food of God's spiritual design, the soul
also gets fed and rightly. We do not
need to provide it with soul-food in

the power of God alone that this birth is
conceived and delivered. (Our freedom to
choose does not empower the act of rebirth;
only God can empower it.) And having been
made in the image of God, so does Man contain
in his species both fatherhood and motherhood.
God separated them for our better
understanding, and because no human being
should ever think himself the equal of God.

addition to spirit-food (or so I sincerely believe). Persons who declare they need to indulge in some recreational activity for the refreshment of soul, saying, "Boy, I really needed that," are mistaken. We are free to do things we enjoy, and God wants us to do so; but to justify doing them as things we absolutely need to do for the sake of our soulish well-being — well, this usually just demonstrates how much our soul is ruling our spirit.

The body also needs its food and exercise to stay in good health, and sometimes we respond with this kind of comment here too. But knocking back hard liquor ("only a couple times a month"), emotional venting through posting online comments hastily or while in a state of negative emotion, video binging, or undisciplined shopping, even window shopping while telling yourself you are being disciplined about your spending, or some other activity performed totally aimlessly and for no other purpose than that one just wanted to enjoy a personal pleasure while willfully indulging in laziness.

Do not mistake my meaning: we are free not to live by strictly established schedules, and are usually the better off for it. And God commands us to rest at times. Most of us don't rest enough. We are also free to explore the world about us for interesting things He created or our fellow souls have been inspired to create. And it is during times of wandering about that God is often taking us somewhere or trying to show us something (or He is trying to get us to practice letting Him do this). But aimless pursuits because we willed to do them — that is, we *determined* to be lazy and *not* to do something more worthwhile, and not really because we needed rest — it is the sense of self that guides these choices. And self and soul are synonymous until the spirit has achieved jurisdiction over all the inner land.

As long as we are diligent to feed the spirit-man, the soul-self will receive its good food too and not feel overly

hungry for what is empty junk food. For
remember, the soul lives with the body
on one side of it and the spirit on the
other and receives what each chooses to
pour into it. Similarly, as long as one
feeds the body those best choices for the
physical frame it can, so also will the
soul receive what it needs of the
physical. Then the soul will naturally receive from the healthy fullness of each
of these, like the rest of the body receives
its nutrients because one puts something into the stomach. As a rule we do
not assimilate nutrients especially for
our hands and feet: what we ingest is
transformed in our body to meet the
needs of our whole frame. Physical
activities engage not only the body, but
also our mind, will, and emotions: we
have to concentrate to some degree on
what we are doing; we have to choose to
do it; and we usually feel something as
we are engaging our self in some
activity. It is that ebb and flow of the
boundaries between the parts: they shift
slightly depending on the season and
the power of the waves, which here are

how much the soul-faculties get incorporated into the physical activities. The same happens when we perform spiritual activities. Are the mind, the will, and the emotions ever not involved when you are in prayer or worshipping God?

To seek out things to nurture the soul—things that deliberately nurture the mind, the will, and the emotions *in themselves*, as though those faculties are the highest we possess—is to me unwise. Anyone can pick up a puzzle book, as especially the elderly do to keep the mind working, and I am not trying to say this is not worthwhile. But I try to live by that old adage (which the Catholic Church is not the only body permitted to use): nihil obstat —*nothing hinders*. But not everything helps.* What

---

* This concept of nothing hindering is also the import of Romans 8:28—"And we know that all things work together for good to them that love God, to them who are the called according to His purpose." God has promised to bring good out of both our best efforts and our most grievous errors because we love Him and sincerely want to be a part of the life of His Kingdom. Yet should we test God by purposely

we choose to be about is often an individual matter because in time we realize what is helpful to us personally and what is harmful to pursuing more profitable activities. What is a stumbling block for you may not be for someone else. Again, legalism doesn't help any-one. It is a spiritual entity that seeks to bind. So you bind it instead and loose anew the spirit of freedom in your life as need be.

So the soul receives in turn what is fed to the spirit and the body. Then everything is pretty much taken care of naturally for the soul just as we live and move and have our being in God* and as we pursue what has been given to us to do. This invariably includes mental exercise for the mind and the nurturing of healthy feeling for the heart. And of course the will gets exercised all day long in even the smallest matters. These things that feed our soul-faculties are

engaging in things we know to be harmful for our self?

* Acts 17:28—"For in Him we live, and move, and have our being; as certain also of your own poets have said, For we are also His offspring."

designed to reach us through everyday activities and encounters with others. That we are always being given opportunities to set our own preferences for things makes it appear that God is just telling us to accept what He offers. And frankly, He often is. Much of the time, though, He does give us choices—not just good or bad, but generously gives us access to comparable choices so that we can pick what we prefer.

As a Loving Parent who is caring for spiritual children of varying ages, those choices vary with stages of development: the less developed, the more restricted the healthy choices; the more developed, the greater the freedom to choose for our self which we would have, because the Father can trust that this child will turn from what it knows to be an unhealthy option. That someone would rather pour out her affection on a beloved celebrity rather than to fill up on spirit-food, is not God's fault. The Lord, say, wants to cause her to encounter her neighbor for the good of them both, but her spirit has no taste for

this because to her manna isn't good
enough if there isn't steak (i.e., flesh)
being served alongside it. She is
choosing not to receive good food for
her soul through this everyday encounter because, in a sense, the taste is
too bland. But her inner system is too
weak to stand richer food because she
would not feed her spirit, and God does
not seek to make His children sick by
meals He knows are too rich for them.

People have largely lost the
knowledge of soul-matters, and so some
of this may sound more complex than it
needs to. Once you set yourself to
seeking God's revelations, He will send
them and they will help you as you
journey along.

For some the soul seems ever to stay in
its terrible-two years. It is in such a soul
especially that it is important not to
overfeed itself soul-food, but it is also
when it is most likely to happen, for the
soul is so underdeveloped that it cannot
comprehend why it should not feed

itself certain things or understand the consequences that might result.

Many do actually develop into spiritual adolescence, but it is less common for souls to develop to full maturity, not because God has not made this possible for the spirit-man—it is far more possible than the number who reach this stage in practice. It is because in the soul, which is ever being tugged back and forth between spirit and flesh, it is much more difficult to gain enough victory over this tugging so that it can be on its way toward the higher road of spiritual living. It is like taking your leave of someone who grabs hold of your jacket and will not release you, who will not cease talking and you don't want to be rude by abruptly interrupting and hurrying away, since you understand he is not doing it to be mean; he just cannot get his mind off himself and his troubles. This is much like how the flesh is forever clutching at the soul and making it very difficult to direct one's being to spiritual things while exerting its strength to be Christlike until it has

opportunity to draw away without
giving offense. Do you want to hate
yourself every time you have some
physical pain or feel sick, as perhaps
you are tempted to hate such needy
persons? But you understand how it is
difficult to pursue God for hours or days
at a time when pain or ailment requires
much time to deal with. No, we gra-
ciously tend to our body's needs at such
times and tell our self, "Tomorrow is a
new day, and perhaps I will be able to
accomplish what I did not today." The
most important thing is to keep pressing
on when you have the chance to do so.

I also cannot seem to forget that God
has decreed death shall be the end of
this flesh — that entity energized by the
fallen self. He has planned to someday
exchange this for a fleshly form energized by His resurrection Life. Presently
we grasp hold of this Life in spirit, and
we are free to receive It throughout the
rest of our nature as our faith enables us
to do.* This transformation is never

---

* Matthew 9:29—"Then touched He their eyes,
saying, According to your faith be it unto you."

forced on us, however, so we can still feel the strong pull of the flesh.*

We must actively choose to permit the transformation into the likeness of Christ — the means by which our faith is enabled to receive more from God — and no one ever promised this was easy. God bless those for whom it is, for God can get right to work using them for His Kingdom. The rest of us have to plod along. So because of this decree of death, it seems to me better just to keep the soul dominated rather than invest much in fixing it. For there is no human means of fixing it. Persons who choose to develop themselves in soul — largely through fleshly means, since they have no access to a living spirit — apart from God's Way only alienate themselves further from Him, especially as they develop more inner power. It is all mind, will, and

---

* You might think every follower would want to partake of this transformation, spirit and body. But I have known a number of sincere believers who were unwilling to relinquish a desire to be emotionally needy or physical invalids. In short, they did not want to let God heal them of the soul-woundedness that manifested in these outward states.

emotions fueling a flesh that has been decreed to die. The stronger the soul's will, the more difficult it becomes to relinquish the soul's will for God's. That is precisely why God instituted a better Way. Many do not want God's Way, however, because it involves that hated dying to self.* They believe (and many do not even really understand what they have done in rearranging the interior parts) that by declaring them-selves a being of body, mind, and spirit, they attend to all their inner needs. But this, as I said, is a misconception.

This knowledge of the soul is necessary as one moves deeper into God, for

---

* Romans 8:13—"For if ye live after the flesh, ye shall die: but if ye through the Spirit do mortify the deeds of the body, ye shall live." *Mortify* means to deaden—to so humble and abase, to crush and put in place and confound efforts to be victorious, that it is as though the effect were death. It is this lifeless after the work of mortification has been completed. This is what Paul teaches is the way to deal with the fallen flesh—that part which is energized by the self. And it is what many souls are offended by. Yet we are free in Christ to become the best person we can be, only energized by resurrection Life rather than the self.

without it, one cannot accurately comprehend what God is pursuing with a
person. Not every soul has to comprehend such truths with mental clarity,
however. Some come to these truths in a
vague way intellectually. They receive
God and accept His presence, and so
they understand experientially the
reality of such things. But if you asked
them to compose an essay on the
subject, they would be hard pressed to
put together two sentences in coherent
language. Yet they may have prog-
ressed deeper into God than one who
has a doctorate in biblical studies because it is spiritual knowledge, not
intellectual. So we must be careful not to
let ourselves believe we can look at a
soul and know where it is in relation to
God, particularly based on educational
levels, either more or less. Discern with
spiritual eyes if it is important that you
do so. Otherwise leave them to God.

So on whatever level it comes,
whether intellectually or experientially
or both, an understanding of the tripartite self is necessary for comprehension

of what it means to progress in spiritual growth and in relationship with God. It not only provides approximate lines between matters of flesh and spirit, understanding also helps discern what may be only of soul and what is of God.

Greater understanding of God always and naturally results in greater understanding of the self. It is actually far more beneficial to concentrate on understanding God than the self, despite the greater complexity of God, for, paradoxically, this is the most efficient way to acquire the self-knowledge needed to proceed. After all, He understands us far better than we understand our self, and He is infinitely more efficient in relaying this information to us than we can be in trying to learn about our self. Excessive introspection never really helped anyone. Occupy yourself with what you have been appointed to do, and the Holy Spirit will guide and reveal regarding the rest. Just be willing to account yourself undeveloped so that God can more fully develop you.

Just the same, it is all still as the child accurately grasping its letters and reading at a primary level. This does not invalidate the knowledge; it only acknowledges its elementary nature. To the child it seems as if mountains are being climbed, its small learning accomplishments seem so great to it. But from God's perspective—well, it is little wonder He still calls us His children, because so we are spiritually. Be kind to yourself as much as to others. We are not transformed into the likeness of Christ in a day.

Remember always that the mountain of feeling is for visiting and the mount of faith is for living upon, and this will guide you when you get off-course, as we all do from time to time.

Even though God does not wish a spirit of confusion to always be dogging our steps in the spiritual life, the truth of the matter is that in the natural realm we are generally unfamiliar with the modes of things in the spiritual, and it takes patience to learn to identify them. Because sometimes it is comforting knowing others have felt too that we are journeying across a strange land, let me leave you with a passage I once read that has come closer than most in describing the nature of spiritual matters while we make our way through the heavy fog of this in-between soul-land:

HERE I interrupt my narrative to remark that it involves a constant struggle to say what cannot be said with even an approach to precision, the things recorded being, in their nature and in that of the creatures concerned in them, so inexpressibly different from any possible events of this economy, that I can present them only by giving, in the forms and language of life in this world, the modes in which they affected me — not the things themselves, but the feelings they woke in me. Even this much, however, I do with a continuous and abiding sense of failure, finding it impossible to present more than one phase of a multitudinously complicated significance, or one concentric sphere of a graduated embodiment. A single thing would sometimes seem to be and mean many things, with an uncertain identity at the heart of them, which kept constantly altering their look. I am indeed often driven to set down what I know to be but a clumsy and doubtful representation of the mere feeling aimed at, none of the communicating media of this world being fit to convey it, in its peculiar strangeness, with even an approach to clearness or certainty. Even to one who knew the region better than myself, I should have no assurance of transmitting the reality of my experience in it. While without a doubt, for instance, that I was actually regarding a scene of activity, I might be, at the same moment, in my consciousness aware that I was perusing a metaphysical argument.

George MacDonald
Lilith, chapter 9

So keep the faith. We all have to make our way through the cloud of unknowing to reach the peak of the Great Rock, the mountain of faith; but the most persistent souls can certainly reach the Mount of God.

May the grace of our Lord Jesus Christ, the love of the Father, and the fellowship of the Holy Spirit be with you always. Amen.